A New & Exact PLAN of the Tow...

John Cossins Map of 1726

"Leeds is a large, wealthy and populous Town - the Cloth Market which is indeed a Prodigy of its Kind and not to be equalled in the World - The Town is very large and there are an abundance of wealthy Merchants in it ....."

So wrote Daniel Defoe in 1724. Defoe's writings are visually confirmed by the "New and Exact Plan of the Town of Leeds" beautifully drawn by John Cossins in 1726. That there was ample wealth based on the wool cloth industry, not yet industrialised, is quite evident when one views the images of the splendid Merchants' houses down each margin.

Whilst medieval Leeds was founded around the Parish Church, the Calls and eventually Briggate, it had not grown greatly by 1726. John Cossins' plan shows the area around Swinegate occupied by the goits and tenters of the wool cloth industry.

And it is in the mid 18th century we commence our Civic Pride Trail tracing the development of Leeds through a brief period of Georgian elegance into the industrial boom times of the Victorian era which witnessed a vast population explosion and elevation to City status in 1893. Our Trail continues into this century with a review of a very impressive Civic Quarter which is grouped around the magnificent Town Hall of 1858, and concludes with a close look at some impressive "monuments of commerce" on and around Park Row.

INTRODUCTION

The extension of Briggate northwards towards St John's Church is indicated and there are open gardens and a Bowling Green west of Lands Lane. However, the town was becoming increasingly crowded and in 1768 the streets were described as being "exceedingly dirty, ill built and badly paved". The wealthier people were beginning to move away from the smoke and smells of towns at this time. Leeds was no exception.

The most desirable places to live would have been to the west of Briggate along Boar Lane around Holy Trinity Church. Impressive Merchants' houses clustered around the Church which was completed in 1726. Cossins' plan includes architectural elevations of three of them. The expansion westwards along Boar Lane was to lead into what we now know as City Square.

Jeffrey's plan of 1770 shows this as the site of the Mixed Cloth Hall, an enormous structure around a central yard. His plan also shows the first general infirmary designed by John Carr and opened in 1771, behind the Cloth Hall.

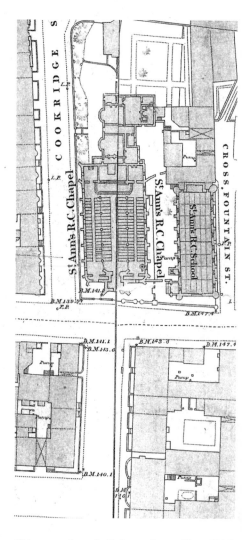

This extract from the Ordnance Survey Map of 1847 and photograph opposite show the original St. Anne's Cathedral which faced out onto the Headrow at the end of Park Row and which was demolished in order to improve traffic flow

Significantly, in 1770 these two buildings are shown as being set within a completely open green space. This space was to be developed with a new planned layout, the Park Estate, bringing to Leeds an urban framework that exists to this day and which retains much of its elegant architectural character.

City Square did not exist in name until 1893. By then the Mixed Cloth Hall and General Infirmary had gone. Having set the historical scene for our Civic Pride Trail it is in City Square that we commence our walk which we hope you will find interesting and entertaining.

Commence in City Square by the Black Prince statue.

A review of the buildings surrounding City Square follows, commencing with the Post Office building with its central clock tower, and continuing around in a clockwise direction.

1 **City Square** (William Bakewell) was opened in 1903 ten years after Leeds was elevated to the status of a city. It originally took the form of an elevated circular podium surrounded by a stone balustrade on which were set the "Morn" and "Eve" statues which were relocated in the 1960's to their present positions with the Black Prince dominating the scene from his high level "saddle". Unfortunately the whole assembly has been dominated by a heavy traffic presence but plans are in hand for the creation of a much more pleasant pedestrian environment. (Further information on the statuary in City Square can be found in the Walkabout Series "Leeds Statues Trail" by Melanie Hall).

2 The **Post Office building** (Henry Tanner 1896) provides a handsome face to the north side of City Square. It stands on the site of the former Mixed Cloth Hall. Note the elaborate treatment around and above the doorways and the skyline parapet features.

Norwich Union's No 1 City Square and the *NATWEST building* form the northern edge of City Square. These contemporary buildings, (commenced in 1996) set opposite each other across Park Row, create a "gateway" into the Leeds financial district. The former with its strongly curved form recalls the shape of the Standard Life Assurance building demolished in the 60's. These buildings are striking recent additions to the city skyline, buildings of quality in both townscape and detail terms.

Mill Hill Chapel (Bowman and Crowther 1847) (plaque). The name suggests the medieval link with the manorial mill by the river downhill from this site. The first home of a Unitarian congregation in 1672, its setting appears somewhat incongruous today, dominated by the adjoining massive Royal Exchange House tower.

Across Boar Lane, the delightful little *former Midland Bank building* (W W Gwyther 1899) whose curved form fits its corner site so well. The green copper dome provides an eye-catching contrast with the backdrop of plain modern structures.

3 The *Queen's Hotel* (W Curtis Green 1937) is by far the largest building in City Square, its massive white Portland stone facade giving strong enclosure to the south side. After much use in London in the 20's and 30's the fashion of using this stone became a popular trend, particularly for major civic and commercial buildings. The present structure replaced the hotel of 1863 built to serve the newly arrived railways to the Wellington and New Stations. Today the current Queen's Hotel serves Leeds City Station which lies just behind. Note the little skyline "temples".

The *former Majestic Cinema* (1921), one of the city's earliest with a basement ballroom. Note the panels of musical instruments at high level.

Having completed the review of City Square, return via the crossing towards the Post Office (note the six listed red phone boxes), and proceed right and then left into Infirmary Street.

Pause to read the plaque on your left, above the door into Cloth Hall Court.

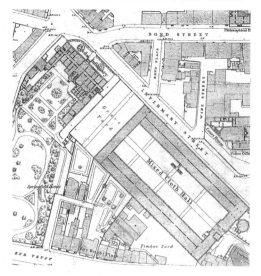

4 The **Mixed or Coloured Cloth Hall** (1756-57) once stood here. The Hall was the largest ever structure built in Leeds arranged around a huge courtyard which could hold 20,000 people for public meetings. It was demolished in 1890.

Carry on until you reach the open area with iron railings on your left.

The *former Yorkshire Penny Bank* (Perkin and Bulmer 1894), This building stands on the site of the first Leeds Infirmary, hence the street name.

The Yorkshire Bank has its origins (1856) in the local savings movement, being entitled the Yorkshire Penny Bank until post-war years. This is one of several buildings in Leeds occupied by the Leeds based group.

This one is a really grand Victorian flamboyant extravaganza! The first Leeds General Infirmary stood on this site, opened in 1771 and designed by John Carr of York.

Proceed to the junction with King Street

Over the road is Devereux House the recently built offices of Eagle Star (1994) with a faintly Scottish Baronial style. Opposite (and in sharp contrast) is *Atlas House* (Perkin and Bulmer 1910) faced in white faience. Note the inventive treatment over the doorway, with Atlas shouldering the globe. This is an excellent example of the use of this glazed and coloured earthenware material, widely used in Leeds from around 1870.

Bear left down King Street, crossing Quebec Street and then King Street. Pause opposite the Metropole Hotel.

5 The *Metropole Hotel* (Chorley and Connon 1899) (plaque) presents a tour de force in terracotta and faience, this time in bright red and pink. The bay windows present some intricate details showing how well clay moulding techniques had advanced by the turn of the 19th century. Although this building uses Welsh materials, the local Burmantofts fireclay industry (situated about 2 miles away on the York Road) was flourishing at this time, exporting to all parts of the world. Note the rooftop cupola. This feature originally crowned the fourth White Cloth Hall, on whose site the Metropole was built. A rare example of Victorian conservation.

If you look down the street to the left of the Metropole you will see a corner of Quebec House, the former Liberal Club, again in similar bright pink terracotta. Gladstone spoke from its tower balcony in 1881

Across the road from the hotel the *Bank of England* (Building Design Partnership 1967) a curious "upside-down" building, stepping out towards the top. Though built with quality materials, it is perhaps hard to imagine how such a building could receive public favour today. The design has its origins in Louis Kahn's Boston City Hall, USA.

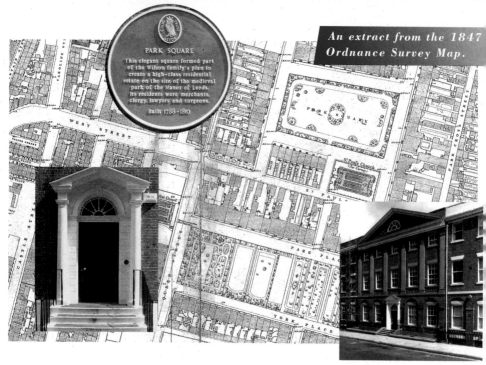

PARK SQUARE

This elegant square formed part of the Wilson family's plan to create a high-class residential estate on the site of the medieval park of the Manor of Leeds. Its residents were merchants, clergy, lawyers and surgeons.

Built 1788-1810

Return to the junction with Park Place.
Pause at the corner.

6 ***Park Place*** is the first of the streets that form part of the Park Estate established by the Wilson family in the late 18th century. The beginnings of conscious town planning began here, ***the "West End" of Leeds,*** introducing elegant terraces, spacious streets and a square. The Estate founded several well-known local highways, Park Row, Park Street, Park Square and Park Place. Things did not quite work out however!

Note the north side of Park Place.

Largely Georgian in style and character (if not in date) it has been spoiled at its east end by the intrusion of modern structures.

But, beyond these, it presents a fine continuous facade uncluttered by extensions. This clean line is formed by many buildings of different types but their proportions, height and glazing patterns provide townscape unity. It seems hard to believe that 200 years ago the residents of this side of Park Place had clear views over green meadows running down to the River Aire.

On the south side of Park Place the scene is quite different. By contrast buildings on this side are higher and specifically built for commercial uses such as warehouses and offices.

Much infill of an ordinary nature has recently taken place (note Landmark House!), but No 3 is one of the best of the Victorian era.

Proceed along Park Place until you reach no 18 on the north side.

7 *This fine house (plaque) is the best in the terrace.* Extensively restored recently the house demonstrates the best that the "West End" could offer. Note the elegant iron railings. To its right No 16 was obviously "modernised" late last century (or earlier this century). This simple brick house has been covered in part by terracotta tiles and window features. The result is harmonious and not too obvious.

Retrace your steps (50 yards or so) to Central Street and turn left. Then cross St Paul's Street, and go along St Paul's Place. Go into Park Square gardens.

8 *Park Square is the most attractive part of the Park Estate.* Built 1788-1810 and largely intact today the square is the finest in the city.

Unlike Bath or Edinburgh New Town there are no grand unified facades, rather a series of well mannered frontages conforming to established building lines. This fashionable place to live did not enjoy long life, however.

Around the turn of the 18th century the Industrial Revolution hit Leeds with a vengeance, destroying a brief period of Georgian elegance.

In particular Benjamin Gott established Park Mills at Bean Ing (site of Yorkshire Post Newspapers now). This enormous structure, the world's first "industrialised" woollen mill (employing over 1200 people), was to prove disastrous to those living in Park Square not far away to the north east. The mills were powered by the newly discovered steam power fuelled by ample supplies of local coal. The prevailing winds carried the dense smoke belching from the mill chimneys across the Park Estate making life a misery for the residents. There were law suits and much litigation but all to no avail. Most left and the character of the area took a downturn. The encroaching tide of industry and commerce had won out. Mercifully however, much of the Georgian built fabric remains.

Now for a review of the buildings that surround Park Square. Go through the north gate into Park Square North to commence a clock-wise walk around the square.

Park Square North provides the best of the facades including several very elegant properties most of which now house professional offices (plaque on No 45).

Park Square East is worth examining for the terracotta entrance feature on No 7, The Chambers, a bit of Victorian modernisation. Further along No 9, Vicarage Chambers presents a more comprehensive treatment.

Park Square South has two large buildings. The first is a neo-Georgian building (note the plaque over doorway depicting its former use as offices for the inland waterways). This stands on the site of St Paul's Church (1793) demolished 1905. The second building is by contrast very much a "landmark" building, certainly deserving to be in any Leeds "top ten".

9 *St Paul's House* (Thomas Ambler 1878) (plaque) for John Barran the man who introduced the ready-made clothing industry to Leeds. This Moorish style warehouse was nearly lost to redevelopment being saved at appeal stage.

Subsequently, it was converted into offices by a complete "gutting" with retention of its facades only. Much of the original parapet and minaret detailing, formerly in terracotta, were replicated in glass fibre. Well worth a close look!

Leave along Park Square West. Pause at the junction with Westgate.

Fowler's plan of 1821 indicates that very little development had taken place across (the then) Park Lane. Moving across the road will take you from the Georgian era into the "Civic Quarter" of Leeds which was developed from some fifty years later (with the Town Hall) and is still evolving. The architectural contrasts, particularly in the scale of buildings, are quite dramatic. From this point can be seen three major buildings of the last 20 years or so.

11 The *Magistrates' Courts* (Leeds Design Consultancy 1990) presents a strong contrast to its "legal neighbour", however. It was designed in the now rather ephemeral Post-Modern style employing multi-coloured brick and some unusual pastel hues for its features. By contrast, the internal spaces are largely white with little strong colour giving an attractive spacious atmosphere.

10 On the right, the *Combined Courts Centre.* Fortress-like in appearance with its splayed blast walls the design is obviously influenced by our contemporary need to secure public buildings against car bombers. Rather a pity that it does not present its entrance to the Headrow and that its large mass is unrelieved by the use of contrasting materials. However, the Centre has a restrained, dignified character that befits its function.

The building has been criticised as "Lego-like" and unsuitable for the dignity of the Law. However, it fits the site well and the corner entrance is in the best Victorian tradition, direct and positive.

12 **Westgate Point** (1982), on the left, is an early example of a building that was broadly described during the 1980s as having the "Leeds Look", a style typified by brick walls and slate roofs.

This style has its critics but this office block was certainly one of the best examples and its mass and form provide a good focal point on a key site at the end of the Headrow and Westgate.

Cross Park Square West towards the Westgate Point offices, then cross Westgate by taking the somewhat

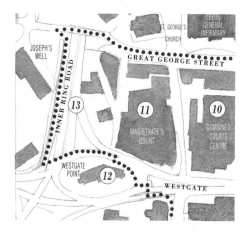

convoluted pedestrian crossing route (shown). Go around the rear of Westgate Point. Cross the first of the two slip-roads turning sharp left up the path between two guard rails. Pause when you reach the bridge over the Inner Ring Road.

13 The **Leeds Inner Ring Road** was built in the mid-60's. Mostly set in cutting or tunnel it describes an almost perfect semi-circular line around the northern edge of the city centre. Now very heavily used it was a prime factor in enabling the city to carry out its pioneering work in pedestrianisation of the central shopping streets 30 years or so ago, a process which continues to this day.

A review of the surrounding buildings from left to right now follows

The office block, **No 2 Park Lane**, is the home of Hammond Suddards, solicitors. In the same materials as many of its contemporaries this building has an unusual facade treatment with its "V" shaped and mirror glass windows, their size no doubt dictated by this very noisy location. Overall a very striking building. Leeds is now said to be the largest legal centre outside London and this practice is one of several who have commissioned their new offices in the city.

To the rear of No 2 Park Lane, *"Joseph's Well"* a former huge clothing factory which is now in multiple business use. This part of Leeds was a traditional location for tailoring firms producing vast quantities of clothing until the 1960's when changes in fashion saw the demise of formal wear such as men's suits.

Straight ahead, beyond the footbridge and above the Inner Ring Road tunnel, are the new buildings of *Leeds General Infirmary*. The Clarendon wing was planned before the Inner Ring Road. was constructed so the road was put into a tunnel, allowing for a considerable expansion of Infirmary and University facilities.

To the right, the massive 1920's buildings of the former Centaur Clothing, behind which lies the original factory, now listed and referred to later.

Proceed towards 2 Park Lane, crossing the slip roads down to the Inner Ring Road. Turn sharp right down the path alongside and above the Inner Ring Road. At the top bear left, then right, crossing over the footbridge. Pause in front of the church.

14 *St George's Church* (John Clark 1836-1838), has a very impressive high level entry at the west end, set above the former crypt. The tower appears squat but it did have a spire, lost in 1962. Locally well known for its sanctuary for the unemployed set up in the crypt in 1930 by the vicar Don Robins. (See "Leeds Places of Worship" by Janet Douglas - Walkabout series).

15 Over Thoresby Place is the highly modelled facade of *Leeds General Infirmary* (George Gilbert Scott 1864-69) (plaque on east gate pillar). This imposing Gothic structure in brick and carved stone was one of the most advanced hospital buildings of its time and followed the principle of having cross-ventilation through separate narrow ward blocks, linked by arcaded pavilions for access.

Across Great George Street from the Church is the original factory of *Centaur Clothing,* its curved corner tower, conical roof and cupola ironwork contrasting with neighbouring buildings.

Proceed along Great George Street, pausing at the junction with Thoresby Place.

Up to your left is the *former Medical School* (W. H. Thorp 1894). This was the second purpose-built facility for the University, in a Tudor-Gothic style, part of the fine medical education tradition that is still developing in Leeds.

Walk along Great George Street past the Infirmary, turn right down the side of the Town Hall. Go up the slope on your left to the front of the Town Hall.

GREAT GEORGE STREET

The great tower and dome were added only in 1857, the result of a change of mind by the Council during construction. That was a crucial change that further enhanced this masterpiece of civic grandeur.

Originally the Town Hall housed Law Courts and the Police headquarters and until 1933 the Council Chamber and Lord Mayor's Rooms. It is famous for its barrel vaulted Victoria Hall, home of the Leeds International Concert Season and Leeds International Pianoforte Competition. A vast organ dominates the Hall's interior (see cover picture).

16 R Leeds Town Hall (Cuthbert Brodrick 1853-58) was the subject of a design competition held in 1852 won by a relatively young and (then) unknown Hull architect. It was opened by Queen Victoria in 1858 amid great celebration and rejoicing, the first time a reigning monarch had visited the town. The Town Hall was a superb demonstration of civic pride and public confidence by the citizens of a very fast growing town. It must have seemed massive compared with the modest structures around. It still retains its dominance despite the competition of the recent office towers to the east.

Brodrick was strongly influenced by the architecture of French Classicism, in fact he retired to that country at the modest age of 47.

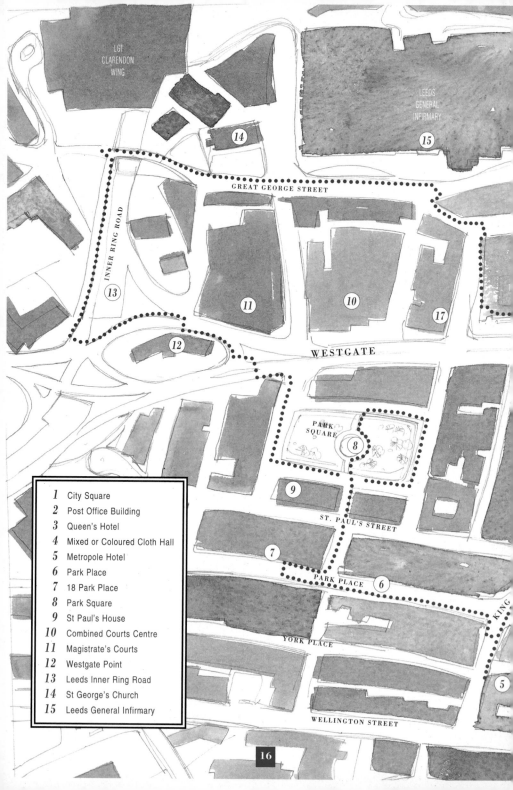

LGI
CLARENDON
WING

LEEDS
GENERAL
INFIRMARY

(14)

(15)

GREAT GEORGE STREET

INNER RING ROAD

(13)

(11)

(10)

(17)

(12)

WESTGATE

PARK
SQUARE

(8)

(9)

ST. PAUL'S STREET

(7)

PARK PLACE

(6)

KING

YORK PLACE

(5)

WELLINGTON STREET

16

1	City Square
2	Post Office Building
3	Queen's Hotel
4	Mixed or Coloured Cloth Hall
5	Metropole Hotel
6	Park Place
7	18 Park Place
8	Park Square
9	St Paul's House
10	Combined Courts Centre
11	Magistrate's Courts
12	Westgate Point
13	Leeds Inner Ring Road
14	St George's Church
15	Leeds General Infirmary

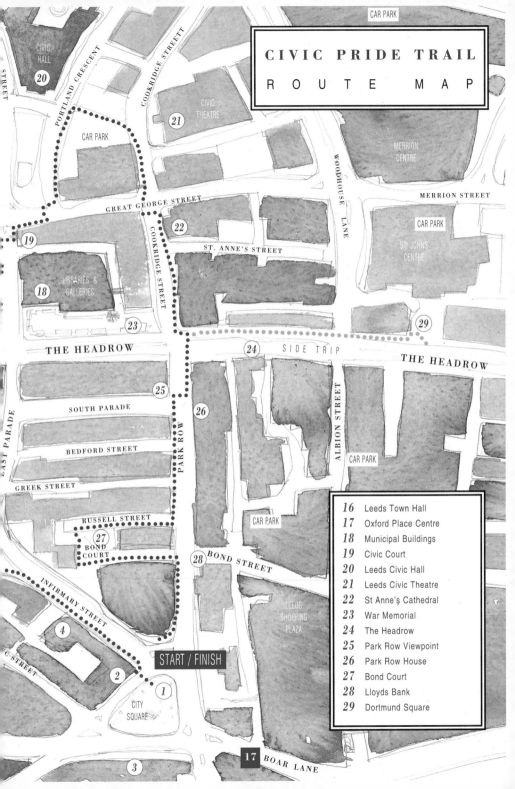

CAR PARK

CIVIC PRIDE TRAIL

ROUTE MAP

CIVIC HALL
20

PORTLAND CRESCENT

COOKRIDGE STREET

STREET

CAR PARK

CIVIC THEATRE
21

WOODHOUSE LANE

MERRION CENTRE

MERRION STREET

GREAT GEORGE STREET

COOKRIDGE STREET

22

ST. ANNE'S STREET

CAR PARK

ST JOHNS CENTRE

19

LIBRARIES & GALLERIES
18

29

23

THE HEADROW

24   SIDE TRIP

THE HEADROW

25

SOUTH PARADE

26

EAST PARADE

PARK ROW

ALBION STREET

BEDFORD STREET

CAR PARK

GREEK STREET

RUSSELL STREET

27
BOND COURT

CAR PARK

28   BOND STREET

INFIRMARY STREET

LEEDS SHOPPING PLAZA

4

STREET

2

START / FINISH

1

CITY SQUARE

16	Leeds Town Hall
17	Oxford Place Centre
18	Municipal Buildings
19	Civic Court
20	Leeds Civic Hall
21	Leeds Civic Theatre
22	St Anne's Cathedral
23	War Memorial
24	The Headrow
25	Park Row Viewpoint
26	Park Row House
27	Bond Court
28	Lloyds Bank
29	Dortmund Square

3

17   BOAR LANE

The media obviously view the Town Hall as the symbol of local government. Its image is regularly seen on national TV networks when the affairs of local government are discussed. There is little doubt that Leeds can be proud to be the home of one of the finest buildings of Victorian Britain.

Before leaving the Town Hall look over the parapet wall on the west side at the Chapel opposite.

17 *Oxford Place Centre (Methodist Chapel)* (J Simpson 1835 but refaced in 1896-1903 by G Danby and W H Thorp) was originally a simple Georgian style structure (as can be seen if you walk around to the west side). However the Chapel was transformed at the turn of the century in a dramatic, almost theatrical, manner with Baroque style additions to the south and east sides.

Walk along in front of the Town Hall, turn left into Calverley Street. Pause at this corner.

18 Across the road the *Municipal Buildings* (George Corson 1878-84) in Italianate style house the Central Library and City Museum. In this case it is suggested that the interior may be of more interest than the outside. The staircases, in particular, in Byzantine Romanesque style, display a wealth of rich materials in strongly modelled spaces, including paired dog carvings on the balustrade.

Walk to the junction with Great George Street and pause to look at three buildings.

19 Across Calverley Street, *Civic Court,* the *former School Board building* (George Corson 1879-81). Like its neighbour by the same architect in Italianate style, the building has recently been extensively renovated and converted to offices. Note the carved stone tablet at roof level and the strongly recessed entrance and staircase. Have a look at the schoolboy and schoolgirl figures just inside the main archway, when you have crossed the road. Corson was apparently criticised for his extravagance on this fine building and was not offered briefs for subsequent Board Schools. However he remained the most prolific of contemporary local architects in commercial commissions.

To your left along Great George Street the *Victoria "Family and Commercial Hotel".* The "Vic" as popularly known was built in 1865 to serve visitors to the Assize Courts with accommodation and refreshment. It retains its attractive frontage after refurbishment.

Next to the Victoria is the *former Masonic Hall* (Perkin & Bulmer 1865), recently renovated for use as a pub, the "Felon and Firkin". Although it was in a terrible condition, a very good rescue was effected. Note the masonic symbols and stone tablet retained at high level.

Cross Calverley Street, turn left and then right around the corner of Civic Court. Cross over Great George Street at the first pedestrian lights. Walk up Portland Crescent pausing by Mandela Gardens on your left.

King George V opened this in 1933 during the Depression, after construction under a public works programme to ease unemployment. Harris was responsible for many other contemporary civic buildings around the country. Controversy arose at the time because of the use of white Portland stone contrasting with the (then) black Town Hall. Recently cleaned, it has some of the qualities of an expensive wedding cake, its twin pinnacles surmounted by seven foot high gilded owls.

Across the gardens to your left the Portland stone faced *Brotherton Wing of the Infirmary* in the bold style of the 1930s masks the Victorian hospital buildings. Note the formerly open semi circular balcony ends on which beds were once placed. So much for fresh air cures!

20 Dominating this space, however, is *Leeds Civic Hall* (E Vincent Harris 1933).

Apart from its main function for local government administration the Civic Hall houses the Council Chamber, Committee Rooms and Lord Mayor's Rooms where civic guests are entertained. There is a splendid Banquet Hall and a display of the City's "treasures" in the superb silver collection, gifts from around the world and many items with Royal associations.

The design, with influences from the work of Sir Edwin Lutyens, respects the dominance of the Town Hall. As one eminent critic puts it ...."the Civic Hall is as ambitious as the Town Hall but not as self confident".

Cross Portland Crescent and take the path through the car park. Pause opposite the Leeds Institute.

21 The *former Leeds Institute of Science and Art (Mechanics Institute)* (Cuthbert Brodrick 1865-68), now Leeds Civic Theatre. Again having strong French influences, the massive strength of this building is indicated by the battered and rusticated base courses and the heavy feel of the stonework above the windows and along the parapets.

Another example of the full height recessed entrance with impressive steps, a device later to be employed by George Corson on civic buildings. The Victorian urge for learning gave birth to many such institutions in towns large and small. Inside, the lecture hall originally accommodated 1500 people. On the plinth to the left can be seen a plaque commemorating Dr Samuel Smiles, the Radical and author of "Self-help". Opposite can be seen the twin gabled *Gothic Shops* designed by Cuthbert Brodrick, nicely restored.

Taking care, cross Cookridge Street, pausing to view plaque and the Gothic Shops. Then proceed down Cookridge Street, pausing at Great George Street to view some interesting buildings at this junction...

22 Across Great George Street, *St Anne's RC Cathedral* (Greenslade and Eastwood.1904) is designed in a simple medieval form, but is obviously influenced by the Arts and Crafts movement. It has a splendid interior with a spacious chancel. Externally, it is a pity that the Cathedral cannot be enjoyed more fully because of its cramped site. However, be sure to look up high to see some wonderful craftsmanship in masonry and sculpture.

Across Cookridge Street, the *former Chorley and Pickersgill Printing Works* (the "Electric Press") with its large arched windows and a good corner entrance with fine ironwork gates. Diagonally opposite, the *"Courtyard"* public house occupies the ground floor of the elegant 3 storey brick terrace, formerly 19th century merchants' houses. The courtyard itself is entered through an archway directly opposite the front entrance to the Cathedral, or from the bar and is a pleasant sheltered space for relaxed refreshment.

You are standing next to the *"Leonardo"* building, which was the offices of the printing works across Cookridge Street and like that building has a dominant corner, but this time with a square angled tower in red brick. This tower has a tiered treatment with elaborate details.

Proceed down Cookridge Street pausing at its junction with The Headrow.

23 Across Cookridge Street the War Memorial (1922) stands in front of the Henry Moore Centre for the Study of Sculpture. This occupies the terrace of former 19th century merchants' buildings along Cookridge Street but the new entrance is on a raised podium facing Victoria Square. Somewhat controversially, the architects chose to face up the exposed gable end with smooth black granite to make a very simple architectural statement.

Architects Jeremy Dixon and Edward Jones designed the Institute and it is the first centre in Europe devoted to the display, study and research of sculpture of all periods and nationalities. It is also the headquarters of the Henry Moore Sculpture Trust. Moore was a local man who was born in Castleford and studied at Leeds College of Art.

The north side was rebuilt after the widening of the narrow streets of the same name which formed the northern boundary of the town in the 18th century.

The new buildings were designed to a master plan by Sir Reginald Blomfield who was responsible for some war memorials in Flanders and for Indian civic buildings. The concept was to create a grand thoroughfare on the model of London's Regent Street. The dual carriageway now has limited traffic flows, only public transport having full through access. The Headrow and Eastgate are an early example of modern town planning, linking Quarry Hill with the Town Hall area.

If time permits you could take a short SIDE TRIP up The Headrow to enjoy the view to Quarry Hill and of the shopping areas. (Directions can be found on page 29). Otherwise, take the following directions.

One of Henry Moore's "Reclining Figures" can be seen on the raised podium and ramp up to the **Leeds City Art Gallery**, just beyond the War Memorial and Institute.

24 **The Headrow** was created in the early 1930s, during the Depression.

Cross over The Headrow, continue down Park Row, then take the first crossing over to the other side. Pause by the pillar box.

Immediately adjacent to the pillar box is Sovereign House, the **former Bank of England** (Philip Hardwick 1864) which faces three streets. A very distinguished example of Classical Revival which has undergone gutting and considerable refurbishment for offices with a wine bar in the former vaults.

26 Across Park Row, **Park Row House** (Alfred Waterhouse 1894) formerly the Prudential Assurance, has recently been beautifully restored. Faced in soft warm brick, terracotta and faience, the Pru was the first building in Leeds to have lifts. This is a really impressive building, probably the best of the older offices in Park Row.

25 **Park Row Viewpoint.** This is a good point from which to see some of the best *"monuments of commerce"* in the city. Mainly Victorian in origin they vary in style and materials.

Park Row is the principal business street in Leeds, home of banks, insurance and finance companies. The varied mixture of buildings is unified by a common height, in the main, with continuous facades.

Next to Park Row House, No 18, *Abtech House* (E. J. Dodgshun 1900) was formerly the West Riding Union Bank. Note the attractive sculpted frieze on which the international nature of banking is depicted, a beautiful example by Joseph Thewlis.

Across South Parade is the former *Scottish Union and National Insurance Companies' Offices* (Perkin and Bulmer 1909) faced in Burmantofts white faience. There are good examples of the quality and versatility of this material to be seen high on this building.

Proceed down Park Row passing ...

On the west side, **31/32 Park Row** (formerly Lloyds Bank, by Alfred Waterhouse 1896), its steeply pitched roof, walls of striped red brick, yellow terracotta and grey granite resembling a French chateau!

Take the first right after passing the "chateau" into Russell Street. Proceed to the centre of Bond Court to view the surrounding buildings.

27 Many fine buildings were lost in the 1960s when the City Council created the **Bond Street Comprehensive Development Area** (CDA) for new offices and car parking. Note the only *"stacker" car park* in Leeds erected to serve the surrounding offices and still functioning. Some of the offices have had a facelift recently somewhat improving their character.

Until 1995, Bond Court was rather bleak and open. Today, however, you will see the beginnings of a *landscaping project* which helps to soften its hard paved nature. The scheme includes a *boules court* where it is hoped local office workers will try their hand at the popular French game whilst enjoying their sandwiches.

Return to Park Row by going up to the right of the Midland Bank. Pause when you get to Park Row.

28 This location was originally a crossroads and in 1928 the *first traffic lights* in Britain were installed here.

Across Park Row the stylish tower of *Lloyds Bank* (1976) can be seen. This is a building of a great quality in design and materials and it fits the corner very well on its raised podium. Set beneath the overhang of the building is Peter Tysoe's famous Lloyds Bank Horse, a powerful image in steel. Lloyds are to be commended for commissioning this fine sculpture and it is a pity that we don't have more such works of art on and around our new buildings.

Turn right down Park Row and enter City Square where you are back at the starting point.

We hope you have found our guide interesting and informative and suggest that you might like to do the walks described in the other Walkabout publications (see inside front cover)

SIDE TRIP

Proceed up The Headrow past Permanent House, the former Building Society offices.

On your left *Headrow Buildings* with local government offices above the shops. Note the fine archway feature above Cross Fountaine Street. Almost opposite this, the *Guildford Hotel* has some good statuary features at first floor level. Before you reach Albion Street you will see on the left at No 44, the *Planning and Building Centre* (the "Planning Shop") where advice and information can be obtained. Copies of the "Walkabout Series" can also be purchased here during normal working hours. Informative window displays may also be seen illustrating planning and environmental issues.

Cross Albion Street, go past Headrow House under its canopy then turn left into Dortmund Square. Pause facing the statue.

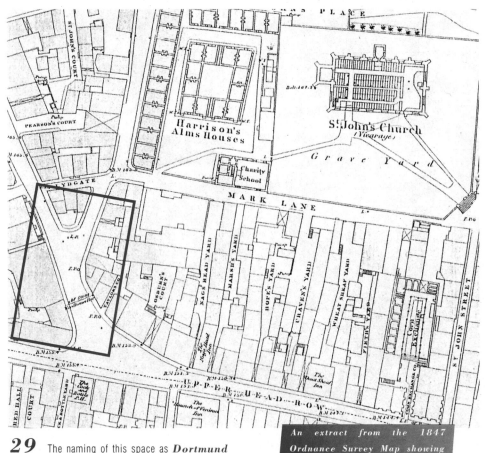

29 The naming of this space as *Dortmund Square* commemorates the long-standing "twinning" relationship with the German city, being inaugurated in 1980 by civic leaders. The *Dortmund Drayman* statue (1980) is a copy of one at a brewery there, beer and lager production being a major industry in that city. The square lies on the major north-south route for pedestrians using the Leeds central shopping areas and is very busy during shopping hours.

Next a review of surrounding buildings.

30

To your left, **Headrow House** a massive brick building has offices at its upper levels. Commenced prior to the Second World War, it was not completed until the 1950's. In front, the **St Johns Shopping Centre** closes the Square to the north. The modern shopping mall has several levels of car parking above, hidden behind the brick banded facade. When open, the Centre gives through access north to the Merrion Shopping Centre.

Across The Headrow behind you, in a post modern style, is the **Headrow Shopping Centre**. It is well worth a visit as it contains a variety of shops and stores of various sizes grouped around a glazed atrium. It stands on the site of Schofield's department store which was a well known local business founded early this century by Snowden Schofield.

On your right, the massive **Allders' Department Store** (formerly Lewis's) built in 1932 as part of the Blomfield plan for The Headrow.

Taking care, proceed to a central point in the Headrow to view longer distance vistas. You are now at the "crown" of The Headrow. To the east, down towards Eastgate, the vista is closed off by the massive bulk of the Government offices, **Quarry House.**

It replaced Quarry Hill Flats (1938), pictured below, once the largest housing development in Europe. Also at Quarry Hill is the West Yorkshire Playhouse and there are ambitious plans for the creation of an Arts campus there.

To the west lies the area you have just traversed. To resume the main walk return to point 24.

Housing the national headquarters of the Departments of Health and Social Security, its design has proved to be very controversial locally.